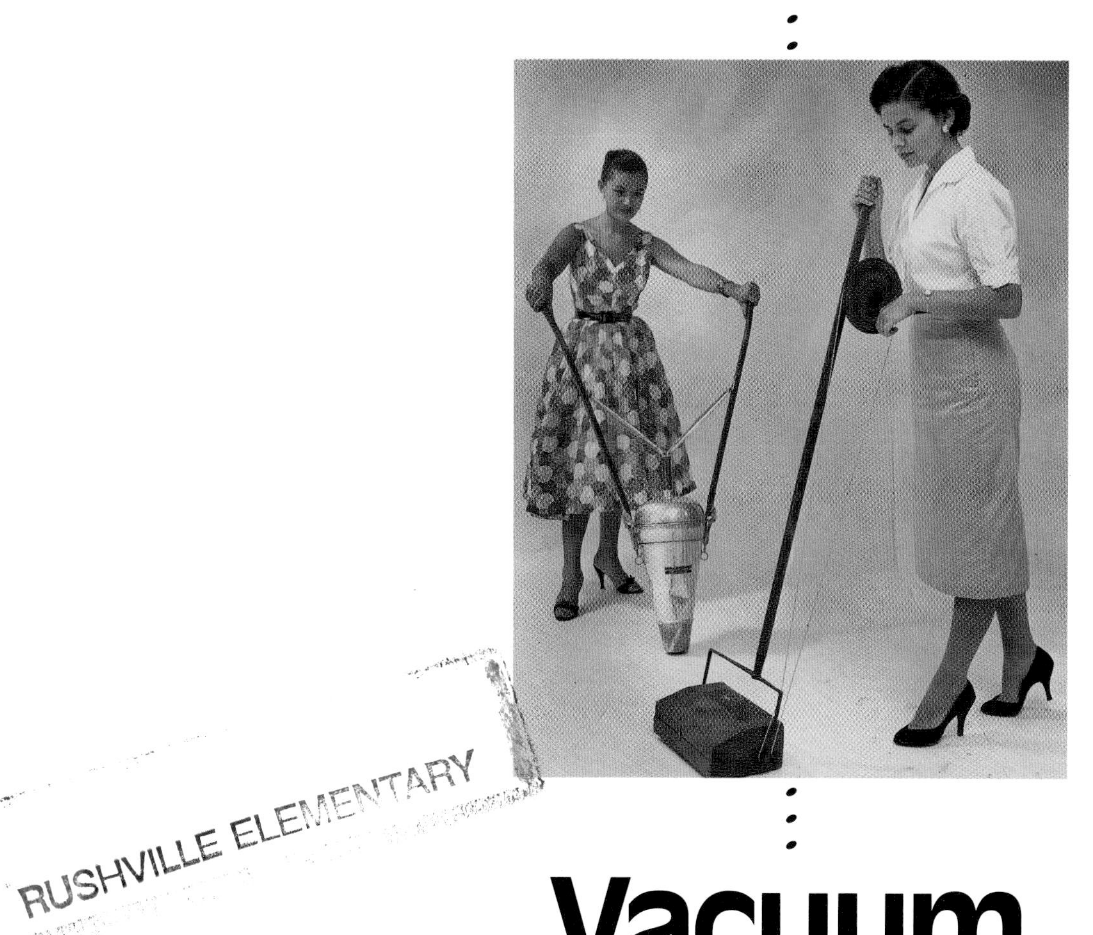



# Vacuum Cleaners

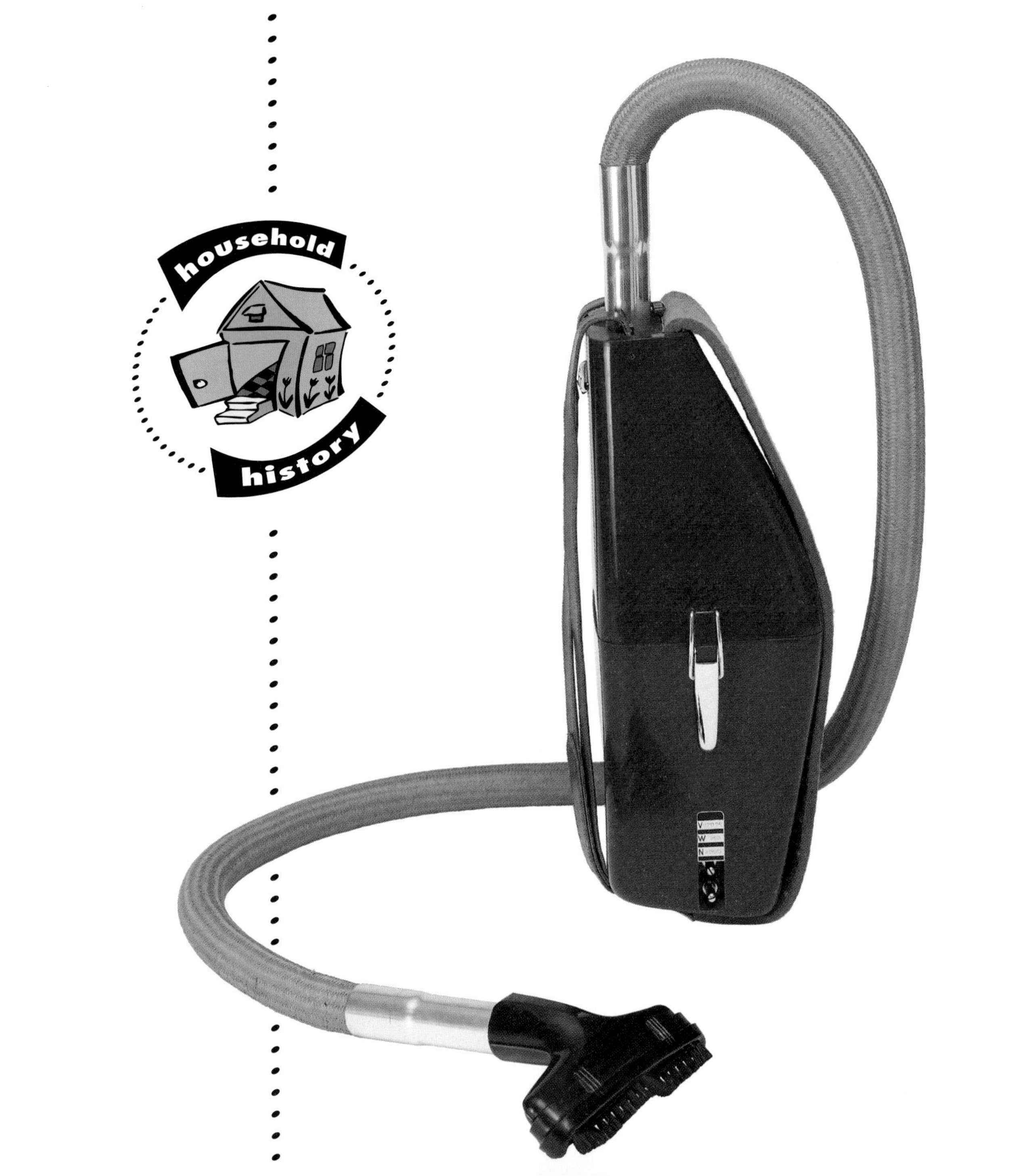
household
history

To Mays Elementary School
Readers –

Have fun cleaning
up the dust of
history!

Your friend,

Elaine Marie Alphin
12 Feb 03

# Vacuum Cleaners

Elaine Marie Alphin

Carolrhoda Books, Inc./Minneapolis

The photographs in this book are reproduced through the courtesy of: UPI/Corbis-Bettmann, cover (upper right), pp. 1, 34; The Hoover Company, North Canton, Ohio, cover (middle right), pp. 6 (upper right), 26, 27, 29 (both), 30 (both), 31; © Jerry Cleveland/Denver Post, cover (lower right), p. 39; Corbis-Bettmann, cover (lower left), pp. 16, 20, 22, 23, 25, 34, 41; IPS, cover (middle left), pp. 3, 17 (upper right); © 1996 The Museum of Modern Art, New York, p. 2; Dyson Dual Cyclone DC01 vacuum cleaner, p. 5; Eureka Vacuum Cleaners, p. 6 (bottom left); Library of Congress, p. 7; U.S. Geological Survey, p. 8 (upper left); © Brian Rogers/ Visuals Unlimited, p. 8 (lower right); NASA, p. 9; © David Scharf/Peter Arnold, Inc., p. 10; Archive Photos, pp. 11, 17, 35; John Erste, pp. 12–13, 44–45; Bissell Inc., p. 19 (both); Archive Photos/American Stock, p. 14; Archive Photos/Hirz, p. 15 (upper left); National Archives, photo no. 83-FB-272, p. 15 (lower right); The Illustrated London News Picture Library, pp. 21, 24; Hollywood Book & Poster, pp. 32, 37 (upper right), 42; Archive Photo/ Statile, p. 33; Andy Freeberg/©1993, The Walt Disney Co. Reprinted with permission of *Discover Magazine,* p. 36; Black & Decker Household Products, p. 37 (upper left); Reuters/ Corbis-Bettmann, p. 38; Purchased with funds from Roy Halston Frowick, Des Moines Art Center Permanent Collection, 1991.46, p. 40; Calvin and Hobbes © 1987 Watterson. Distributed by Universal Press Syndicate. Reprinted with permission. All rights reserved, p. 43.

*For Art, who accepts our vacuum cleaner's rare excursions outside the closet*

Words that appear in **bold** in the text are listed in the glossary on page 46.



Carolrhoda Books, Inc., c/o The Lerner Publishing Group
241 First Avenue North, Minneapolis, MN 55401 U.S.A.

Library of Congress Cataloging-in-Publication Data

Alphin, Elaine Marie.
Vacuum cleaners / Elaine Marie Alphin.
p. cm. — (Household history)
Includes index.
Summary: Discusses the history and technical development of the vacuum cleaner, from the first carpet sweepers of the nineteenth century to twentieth-century improvements.
ISBN 1-57505-018-8
1. Vacuum cleaners—History—Juvenile literature. I. Title. II. Series.
TX298.A55 1997
683'.83—dc20 96-36457


Manufactured in the United States of America
1 2 3 4 5 6 - JR - 02 01 00 99 98 97

# Contents



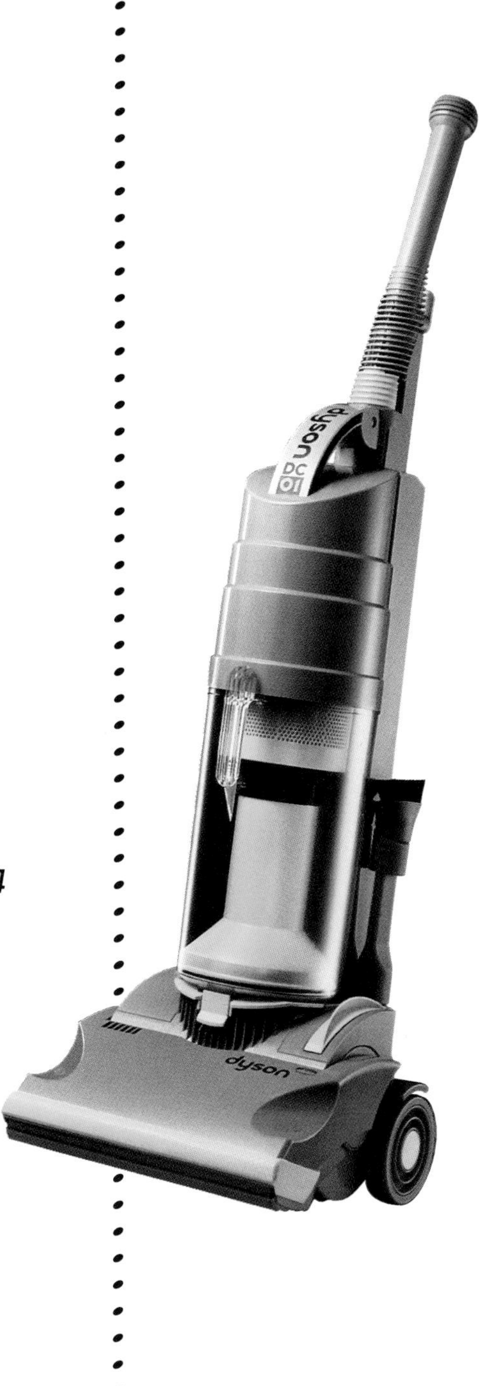

# Up to Your Nose in Dust

VROOM—VROOM. That roar sounds promising. Is it the space shuttle blasting off? Or a tank charging across the front lawn? Afraid not. It's really the hall **vacuum cleaner** revving its engine, eager to start the war against dust.

There's a reason why parents make kids vacuum their room every week. If kids don't want to be buried in dust, they have to do something about it.

During the 1930s, dust storms swept through the southern Great Plains states. Parts of Kansas, Colorado, New Mexico, Oklahoma, and Texas became known as the Dust Bowl. Dust storms continue to happen around the world in dry areas with few plants to keep soil from eroding.

The air around us is full of dust. Dust is any sort of microscopic particle that can be suspended in the air. Carbon from car exhaust makes up a lot of the dust around us. Smoke from factories and coal-fired electric plants makes up even more. But dust can be particles of nature, too. It might be bits of dry soil blowing in from the backyard, or pollen from weeds, grasses, and flowers. Sometimes dust can be dander from cat or dog hair. Dust can even be bits of human hair and skin, or tiny pieces of insect bodies and insect eggs. Gravity pulls all this dust out of the air.

*Volcanic eruptions produce a special kind of dust formed from lava.*

## The Dust Pileup

Scientists believe that more than 43 million tons of dust fall over the United States every year. In a big industrial city, as much as 200 tons of dust could settle each month on a square mile. In a small town, it might be as little as 25 to 50 tons of dust every month. But even in the cleanest town, that comes to nearly a ton of dust settling on one square mile each day of the year.

Much of that dust settles outdoors, but a lot of it gets into the house. Dust can come in through open doors and windows. A screen may keep out flies, but dust slips right in. Walls may be solid, but a house is rarely airtight. On a windy day, there's often a draft around windows and doors.

*A dust devil, a whirlwind filled with dust, zips across a dry riverbed in South Africa.*

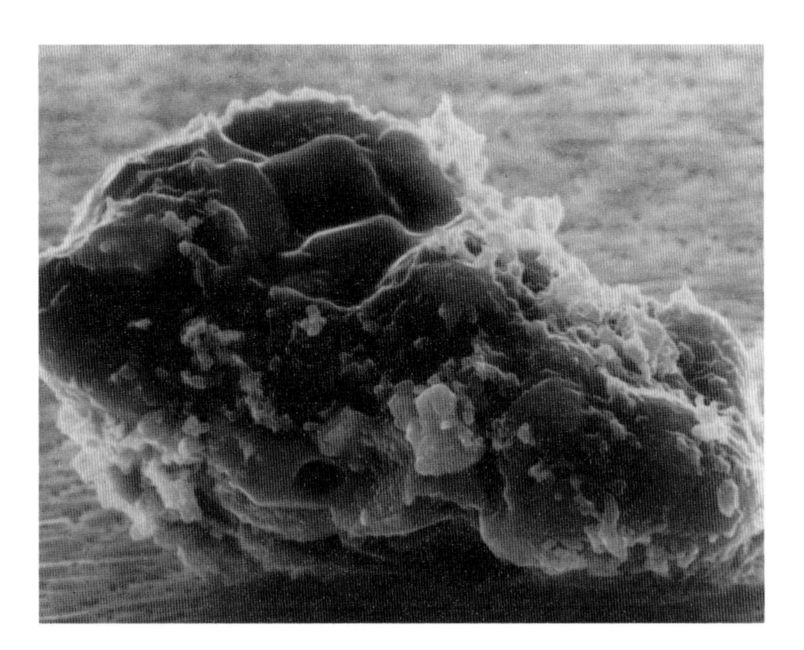

*Dust is all around us; some even comes from space. This piece of microscopic space dust (magnified 15,000 times) is what scientists call a micrometeorite. It may have once been part of a comet.*

That draft is carrying dust inside. Some dust, such as ashes and exhaust, may even be produced inside the house. In fact, indoor air usually contains about twice as much dust as the air outside. That's a million microscopic particles in a cubic inch of air!

If you look closely, you'll discover that dust is full of living things. Bacteria, viruses, mold spores, and fungi are all found in dust. Dusty mattresses, pillows, and sofa cushions can create a home for tiny creatures called **dust mites.**

*About 2,000 dust mites can live happily in one ounce of mattress dust. This household dust mite has been magnified 200 times.*

These microscopic, insectlike creatures eat the dead scales of human skin that are shed naturally every day.

The idea of tons of dust and hungry dust mites piling up on every surface is bad enough. What's worse is that many people, including kids, are allergic to pollen, spores, dander, and especially the waste products of dust mites. Unless something is done about the dust on a regular basis, people may have violent allergic reactions. Some people sneeze or have red, watery eyes. Others might have a runny nose, shortness of breath, or asthma attacks. And some people have *all* of these reactions.

## Vacuum Attack!

The best way to fight back against dust is to use a vacuum cleaner. Vacuum cleaners work by sucking air through a hose into a bag. This bag has a very fine **filter** that traps dust inside but lets clean air pass through. When the switch on a canister vacuum cleaner is turned on, an electric motor drives a fan that pulls air from the nozzle through the hose and then through the filter.

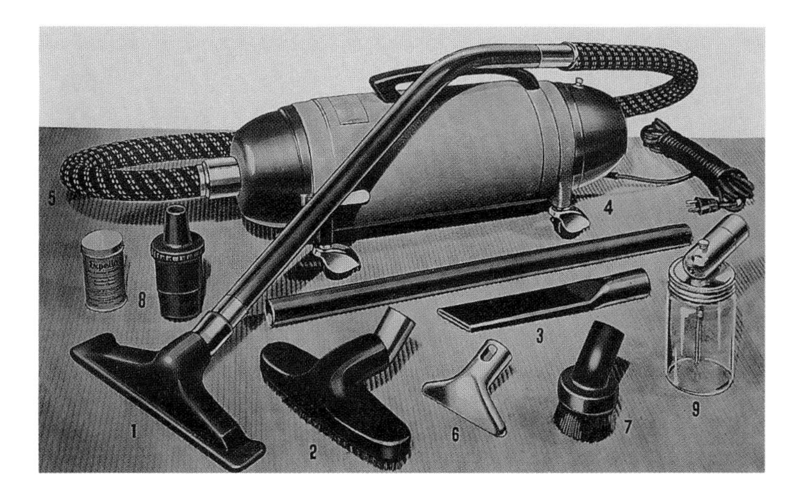


*A typical canister vacuum cleaner, with its many attachments*

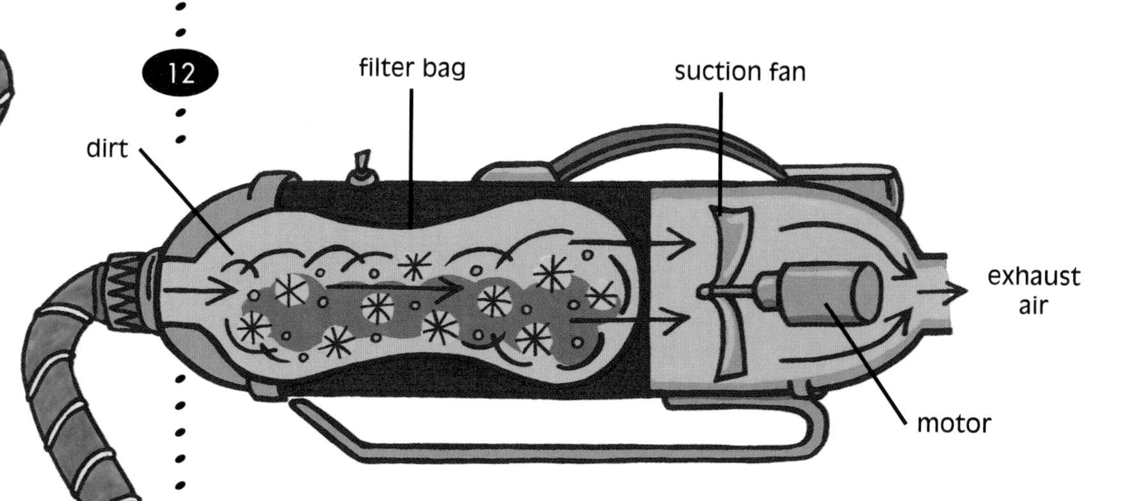


As the fan pulls air through the hose, it creates a **vacuum.** A vacuum is a space from which some or all of the air normally present has been removed. In a vacuum cleaner, air pressure inside the hose is less than air pressure outside the hose. The greater pressure outside forces air packed with dust up into the empty hose in an attempt to equalize the pressure. The motor continues to drive the fan, however, so the dusty air is pulled into the bag. The air passes through the filter and back into the room's **atmosphere,** while the dust remains in the bag. The hose is again empty and at a lesser pressure than the atmosphere outside. This process continues until the vacuum cleaner is turned off.

Upright vacuum cleaners operate much the same way, although they don't have a visible hose outside. The motor in an upright vacuum cleaner drives both a fan and a beater bar. This bristle-covered bar revolves at the mouth of the vacuum cleaner. It tugs up the carpet fibers and beats the dust up and out. The hose opening is inside the base of the cleaner, and the beater bar whisks the dust toward the mouth of the hose. Then the difference in pressure sucks the dust and air up into the hose and on into the bag.

The vacuum cleaner makes controlling dust a lot easier, even if it takes a person to flip on the switch and push the machine around the room. But there was dust long before there were vacuum cleaners. What did kids do back then when their parents made them clean their room?

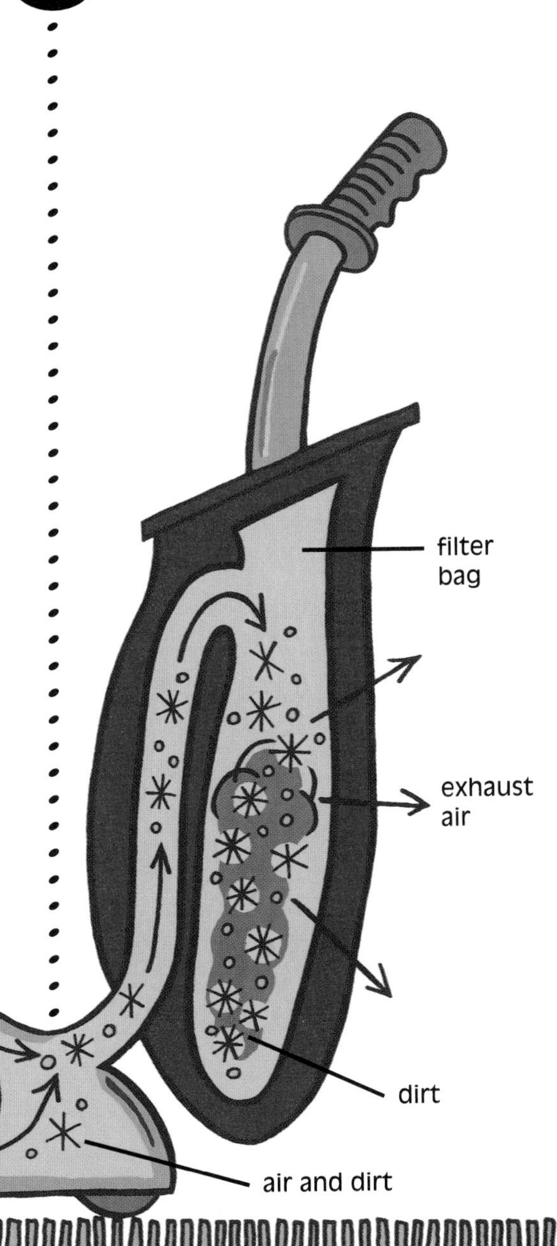

# The Broom and Sweeper Breakthrough

*Brooms, in various forms, have been a handy tool in the war against dust for thousands of years.*

Ever since prehistoric men and women learned to pull branches off trees, people have been sweeping their floors. Most brooms were simple affairs, made from several branches tied together. Better brooms were made from a bundle of twigs tied to a long stick for a handle. This style of broom was the main tool of housecleaning until the mid-1800s.

*Made from broomcorn, a type of sorghum, brooms move dirt around so that it can be disposed of more easily.*

## Sweeping America

In 1850 an American farmer came up with the idea of taking the stiff tuft on the top of a stalk of **broomcorn** and using it for a brush. This discovery started a new industry. The first factory making brooms from broomcorn was opened in 1859 by Ebenezer Howard at Fort Hunter, New York. Business flourished. By the 1890s, American factories were turning out 36 million brooms a year.

*In this photograph from the 1890s, African-American plantation workers use handmade brooms.*

*Deep-down cleaning, in the days before vacuum cleaners, often meant getting down on your knees and scrubbing by hand.*

The problem with a broom was that it only swept dust from one place to another. A broom couldn't catch and hold dust so that it could be disposed of. Dust could be swept into dustpans, but this only worked for the dust that the person who was sweeping could see. Dirt and ash were easy to see, but the microscopic particles that made up most of the dust were invisible. The broom swept the dust on the floor, while the unseen dander, spores, pollen, and dust mites were flung into the air to settle back down again.

To get around this problem, some housekeepers dipped their brooms in water. Damp bristles trapped dust and made it easier to get dust into the dustpan. Serious housekeepers used damp cloths and hand brushes to clean floors properly. This sort of regular washing kept the dust invasion under control.

But what about rugs and carpets? Very few homes had carpets before 1850. Some had small rugs, and these were washed regularly. Between washings, housekeepers took rugs out and hung them on a line. Then they beat the rugs with a tool that looked like a large flyswatter. Housekeepers also washed and beat blankets and curtains to fight off dust.

As more and more people bought carpets, demand grew for a better way to clean them. More effective **carpet beaters** came on the market, but it was quite a chore to carry heavy carpets out for regular beatings. Housekeepers wanted something better.

*Cleaning carpets wasn't always just a matter of flicking a switch and running a vacuum cleaner over the rug. For smaller carpets, people used handheld carpet beaters (above). For larger carpets, only an industrial strength carpet cleaning machine (left) would do.*

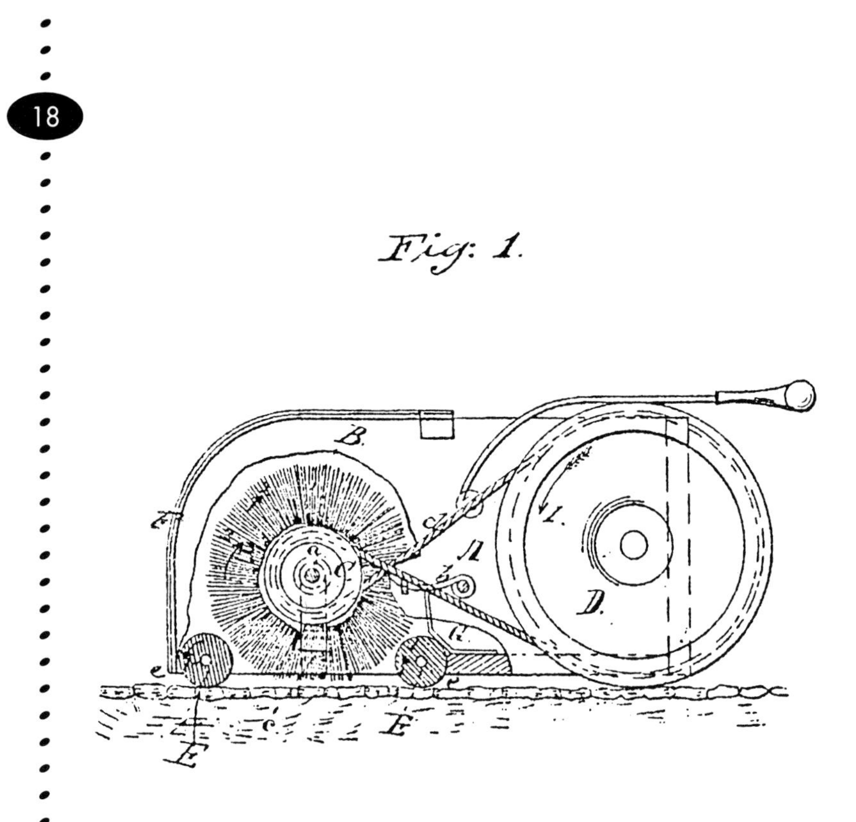


*This American street-cleaning machine is typical of early experiments that led to the development of carpet sweepers and vacuum cleaners.*

Part of the answer to the problem came from England. In 1699 Edmund Heming had invented a street-sweeping machine mounted on a horse-pulled cart. A large circular brush revolved beneath the cart, throwing up dust and dirt from the street. Heming's invention was better than a broom, but it still could not capture dust.

In 1811 James Hume borrowed Heming's revolving brush idea. He put the brush inside a box with a broomstick handle attached. Now it could clean floors and trap dust in the "dustpan" inside the box. Lucius Bigelow introduced an improved model in 1858, and H. H. Herrick copied this English sweeper in Boston. However, the Civil War began just as Herrick's sweeper was growing popular. His employees joined the army, and Herrick could not keep producing his sweeper.

## "Bisselling"

Anna Bissell of Grand Rapids, Michigan, got one of Herrick's sweepers, but she wasn't satisfied with it. She and her husband, Melville, owned a crockery shop where shipments of china and glass came packed in sawdust. Anna wanted a sweeper that would pick up the sawdust, but the Herrick sweeper scattered most of it in the air. Melville Bissell began tinkering with the original **carpet sweeper** design. Before long, he came up with a new machine whose brushes could be adjusted to the sweeping surface.

In 1876 Anna was the proud owner of the one and only Bissell carpet sweeper. Then a customer saw Anna using it and wanted to know where she could buy one, too. After more customers asked, the Bissells started making carpet sweepers. In time the crockery shop closed, but the Bissell carpet sweeper factory flourished.

*Above: Anna Bissell*
*Below: The Bissell crockery shop*

*"Bisselling" was a simple chore compared to beating carpets.*

When Melville died in 1888, Anna went on to run the company. She began exporting carpet sweepers to Europe and Asia. Queen Victoria chose Bissells to clean her palace, and **"bisselling"** became a housecleaning verb in England.

The Bissell carpet sweeper was the best answer yet to the dust problem. But it still failed to capture all the dust and dirt lodged deep in carpets and upholstery. Was there another way to deal with dust?

## Mr. Booth Inhales

Several inventors thought there might be a better way. In the 1890s, some Americans started blowing **compressed air** into carpets to stir up dust. The idea was to force dusty air out of carpets and into a large metal box. H. Cecil Booth was a young English inventor and engineer who designed bridges. He saw a compressed air machine demonstrated at London's Empire Music Hall in 1898. As with earlier brooms and sweepers, this machine blew a lot of dust and dirt into the air. Why blow air into carpets? Booth wondered. Why not suck up dusty air instead?

Booth discovered that this idea had been considered, but it had never worked. Certain that **suction** was the answer, Booth tried a little experiment in a restaurant. Ignoring the shocked expressions of the waiters, he pressed his mouth against an apparently clean plush seat back. He inhaled with all his might—and choked on a mouthful of dust.

Booth was more convinced than ever that suction was the answer. The problem, he realized, was finding the right kind of filter. The perfect filter would allow air to pass through but would trap dust.

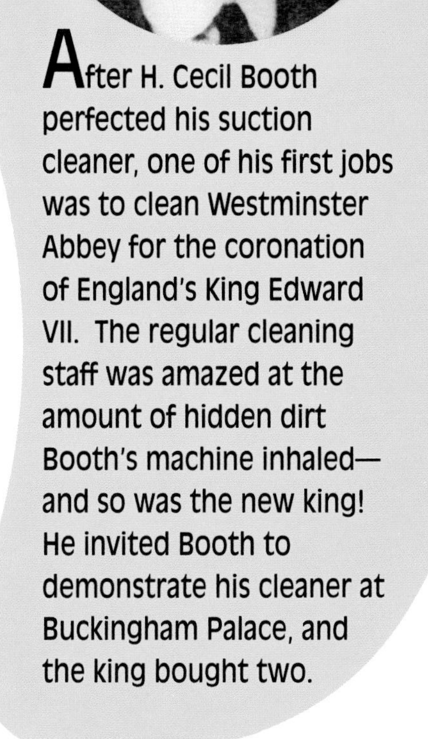

After H. Cecil Booth perfected his suction cleaner, one of his first jobs was to clean Westminster Abbey for the coronation of England's King Edward VII. The regular cleaning staff was amazed at the amount of hidden dirt Booth's machine inhaled—and so was the new king! He invited Booth to demonstrate his cleaner at Buckingham Palace, and the king bought two.

At home Booth lay on the floor on his stomach and experimented by inhaling dust from his carpet through different kinds of fabric. To his surprise, a tightly woven cotton handkerchief allowed him to breathe clean air. On the other side of the cloth was a dusty smudge.

In 1901 Booth patented an electric motor-driven suction cleaner. His invention took advantage of the spread of electricity to public buildings and even to some large homes.

*Early vacuum cleaners weren't exactly portable or easy to use. This model was powered by coal and required a staff of three to operate it.*

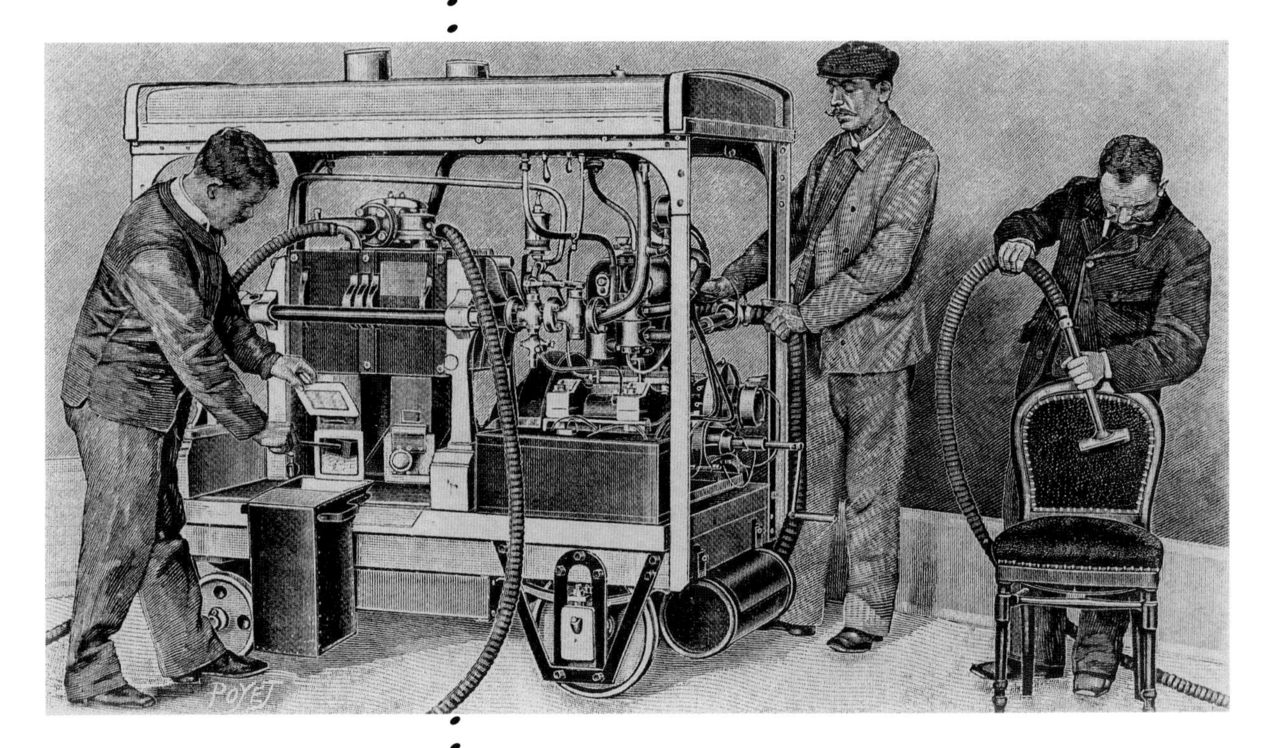

Several American inventors experimented with suction cleaners. Some of these cleaners used a **bellows** to create suction. Housekeepers pumped the bellows by hand as they pushed the cleaner across the carpet. These bellows cleaners worked without electricity and created steady, though weak, suction. But they often took more muscle power to operate than a carpet sweeper or broom.

*An elegantly dressed woman bravely attempts to clean her rugs with a bellows-type vacuum cleaner. Such cleaners generally required lots of strength.*

Early home vacuum cleaning systems were so expensive that only the rich could afford them. In this photograph, a maid uses an electric-powered suction cleaner. Although she is shown here cleaning walls, some early advertisements showed a maid or butler vacuuming the master of the house—or at least the master's suit!

David Kenney's large-scale suction cleaner was more successful. Using his skills as a plumber, Kenney designed a foot-wide nozzle connected to a three-quarter-inch hose. The hose led back to a suction pump and filter. Kenney patented his invention in 1907. He went on to install machines in the basements of homes, hotels, and other buildings. Pipelines connected the machine to outlets in each room. To vacuum a room, the maid or janitor hooked the cleaning nozzle to an outlet.

*Those without a basement-model cleaner could call on traveling vacuum cleaning services.*

These machines were still a long way from the portable vacuum cleaners people now use. It took an inventor who suffered from allergies to dream up a lightweight machine everybody could use.

# The Vacuum Cleaner Takes Off

*For James Murray Spangler, coming up with a better way to clean dust and dirt was almost a matter of life or death.*

James Murray Spangler had always liked inventing things. He had invented a velocipede wagon and a hay rake that not only lifted a swath of hay but also combined it with another one. Unfortunately, his inventions never seemed to make much money, so he needed a regular job to support himself.

Times were hard in Canton, Ohio. The only job Murray could find was as a janitor in the Zollinger Department Store. Spangler's main job was to push an industrial version of the Bissell carpet sweeper along carpeted aisles. However, only a small part of the billows of dust seemed to go inside the sweeper. Most of the dust went up Spangler's nose.

## A Sweeping Solution

Spangler needed the job, but he was allergic to dust. Soon his sneezing and coughing were so bad that he knew he'd have to do something about the dust or quit his job. As an inventor, he was sure he could come up with a better method of cleaning. His first idea was to put the motor from an electric fan on the sweeper brush to make the machine easier to push. This worked too well. The power-driven brush threw up even larger clouds of dust.

But Spangler saw that his idea could work. He decided to experiment with using the fan to pull air and dust into a pillowcase. This worked well enough to show him that he was on the right track. Spangler made a roller brush from goat bristles (the stiff hairs that grow on the back and sides of the goat). He stapled them to a piece of broom handle. Using tougher metal, he built a stronger fan and let the original fan motor power it. Then he carefully attached his fan and motor to his pillowcase dust bag and goat bristle brush. Finally, Spangler sealed everything inside a wooden soap box with adhesive tape to make it airtight.

*This early Spangler cleaner has a pillowcase dust bag.*

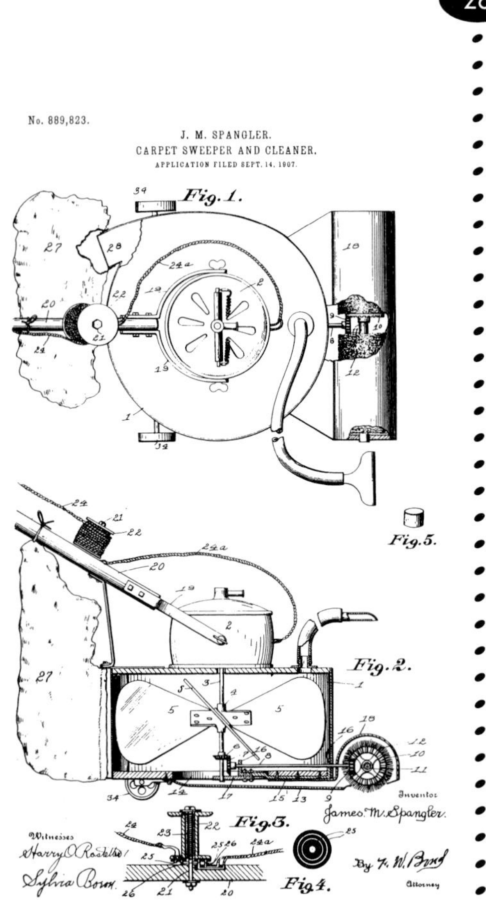


*Spangler filed his patent application in 1907 and then eagerly awaited its approval.*

Murray Spangler's suction sweeper was a huge success. Not only could he work without coughing, but he also spent less time cleaning. That left him plenty of time to think about better methods of producing his machine. Perhaps this was the invention that would make money for him at last.

Spangler patented his invention on June 2, 1908. He raised what money he could from his friends to buy parts and supplies. Then, with high hopes, he began producing his electric suction sweepers. Unfortunately, he found selling harder than inventing. But while he hadn't asked his family for money, he didn't mind asking them to buy his invention.

Spangler called on a cousin, Susan Hoover, and demonstrated his machine in her home. She was so delighted with it that she immediately bought one. Her husband and sons were less impressed. Her son Herb warned her, "Mother! You've been taken to the cleaners by the cleaners!" But Mrs. Hoover was convinced that she had made a wise purchase.

Her husband, William Hoover, was in the leather tanning business. For years his tannery had made horse collars, saddles, and other leather goods. However, with the invention of the horseless carriage, Mr. Hoover could see that business was going to suffer. At the same time that Spangler was wondering how to make his latest invention a success, Hoover was looking for a way to move his company into the new century.

*Susan Hoover*

*Left: A woman demonstrates one of Spangler's first models.*

*The Hoover Company, in its tannery days*

Hoover and Spangler agreed to go into business together. Spangler would work on production, research, and development. Hoover and his sales force would sell the electric suction sweeper. And Herb, who was afraid that his mother had been taken to the cleaners, became general manager of the new cleaner division.

Because suction was created by a vacuum in the hose, the new machine became known as the vacuum cleaner. The Hoover Company marketed the machines on a ten-day free trial basis. That way, people could use the cleaners in their homes without having to pay anything in advance. People tried them doubtfully at first, but they were so delighted with the cleaners that they almost never returned them. Salesmen demonstrated the machines in the home of anyone who was interested, and sales began to build.

*Right: The suction sweeper that took Hoover out of the tannery business and into a new age.*

## The Competition Arrives

Business was so good, in fact, that other manufacturers got in on the action. In 1910 in Cleveland, Ohio, James Kirby invented a cleaner that not only vacuumed carpets but also used water to take dirt out of the air. Kirby next developed a broomstick model with a special switch to cut off the waterline, allowing him to connect different attachments.

The biggest problem the Hoover sales force faced was that the cleaners were simply too good. Where were the familiar clouds of dust? When housekeepers used a broom, cleaning progress could be measured by the satisfying billow of dusty air. But it was hard to see where the dust went when it disappeared inside the filter bag. When the bag was emptied to show how much dirt had been sucked up, some people were even insulted. They refused to think they could have that much dirt in their homes!

Just as James Kirby was introducing his vacuum cleaner, Fred Wardell was looking for a way to break into the cleaner business. When he got a job selling cleaners for the Stecher Electric and Machine Company in Detroit, Michigan, he said, "Eureka!" That's the Greek word for "I have found it!" It was also the name Wardell gave to Stecher's new vacuum cleaner line.

Because vacuum cleaners were fairly expensive, Wardell came up with a new idea. He let his customers take Eureka cleaners home and pay on installments. By 1927 the Eureka Company was selling twelve million dollars' worth of vacuum cleaners each year.

*Kirby, a character in the animated film* The Brave Little Toaster, *is based on Kirby cleaners.*

## Innovation and Change

Gustave Brachhausen, a German immigrant, had started the Regina Music Box Company in Rahway, New Jersey, back in 1892. His music boxes (about the size of a modern large-screen television) were made beautifully by hand. But when Thomas Edison invented the phonograph only five miles from Brachhausen's factory, business didn't look so good. New record players began to replace music boxes in people's homes. By 1919 Brachhausen was out of the music box business. Instead, Brachhausen's Regina Vacuum Cleaner Company was perfecting its cleaners. In 1929 the company added floor polishers to its line of canister and upright vacuum cleaners. Regina later developed the lightweight Electrikbroom.

This was not the only competition Hoover faced. At the same time American inventors were experimenting with suction cleaners, inventors abroad were making their own changes.

*Introduced in 1934, the Electrikbroom recalls the shape of early bellows-type suction cleaners.*

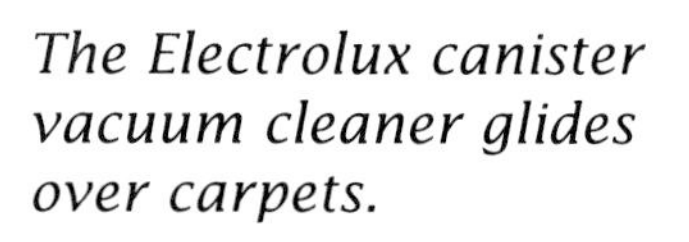

*The Electrolux canister vacuum cleaner glides over carpets.*

In the 1920s in England, Booth began making small cleaners, called Goblins. In Sweden a company called Aktiebolaget Elektrolux developed a new line of vacuum cleaners that took that country by storm. Unlike the large, bulky upright cleaner, the Electrolux's small cylindrical tank slid over carpets on gliders instead of wheels. Its long, flexible hose could clean furniture and draperies as well as floors.

Gustaf Sahlin brought the first Electrolux cleaner to New York in 1924. He set up a door-to-door sales campaign that soon employed over ten thousand men and women. This was among the first sales forces to employ women. Before long, the Electrolux was as popular in America as it was in Europe.

With all this competition, Hoover had to make some changes. Listening to customer feedback, the Hoover Company moved the wheels farther back on the upright model. This allowed suction to work across the entire width of the cleaner. It also made the machine more useful on stairs and in corners. In response to another customer request, Hoover added a light to the vacuum cleaner. This light was mounted on the front of the machine so that people could see under furniture and even clean their carpets in the dark.

*A happy owner of a Hoover vacuum cleaner shows off the many attachments and the innovative light.*

*Frank Jenkins, of Menlo Park, California, is trying to program a vacuum cleaner to clean all by itself. His "Homer Hoover" is a robotic vacuum.*

## Vacs of the Future

The vacuum cleaner's design and function have not changed much since Booth and Spangler set the standards. From 1940 to the present, inventors have built on these basics to compete in the cleaning industry.

One new way to control dust is to "bust" it with Black & Decker Dustbusters. Handheld, cordless, rechargeable Dustbusters are great for sucking up a trail of crumbs or for using in a place with no electricity.

*Black & Decker advertises that its Dustbusters will do just that—bust dust.*

In the 1990s, Matsushita introduced a "smart" vacuum cleaner. It uses a light sensor to measure the dirt being sucked through the hose. The cleaner automatically changes its suction power to match the amount of dirt. There are even electronic air-filtering vacuums inspired by space program technology. These machines use HEPA (short for High-Efficiency Particulate-Arresting) filters to remove up to 99 percent of dust particles in the air.

Bissell introduced the Big Green Machine in 1992 for big cleaning jobs. This vacuum cleaner forces a cleaning solution into dirty carpeting or upholstery. Then it uses suction to pull the dirty cleanser back into a tank.

*The first vacuum cleaner in space was a character on the animated television show,* The Jetsons.

*The French have harnessed vacuum cleaner technology in their own ways, using it to scoop animal refuse from the sidewalks of Paris.*

## Beyond the Home

Modern vacuum cleaner technology isn't limited to housecleaning. French designers may have been thinking of the Big Green Machine when they created scooters with vacuum cleaners attached to them. These scooters patrol French streets on the lookout for dog poop. A cleaning solution whirls the animal droppings into a holding tank and disinfects the sidewalk all at the same time.

*Vacuum cleaners even help move prairie dogs off ranch land.*

In California, strawberry growers use a huge vacuum cleaner they call "bugvac" to suck bugs from their plants. And in Colorado, Gary Balfour uses a vacuum cleaner with a 50-foot-long hose to suck prairie dogs out of their underground burrows. He transports the animals to new locations, while making ranch land safe for horses and cattle.

Booth and Spangler would probably be surprised at some of the ways vacuum cleaners are used today. But they might be even more surprised if they could see how much vacuum cleaners have changed people's lives.

Vacuum cleaners turn up in many surprising places. At airports, a kind of vacuum cleaner is sometimes used to detect drugs and explosives. When bombs or drugs are hidden in suitcases, microscopic traces stick to the outside. A modified vacuum cleaner sweeps over each suitcase, looking for traces that mean drugs or bombs.

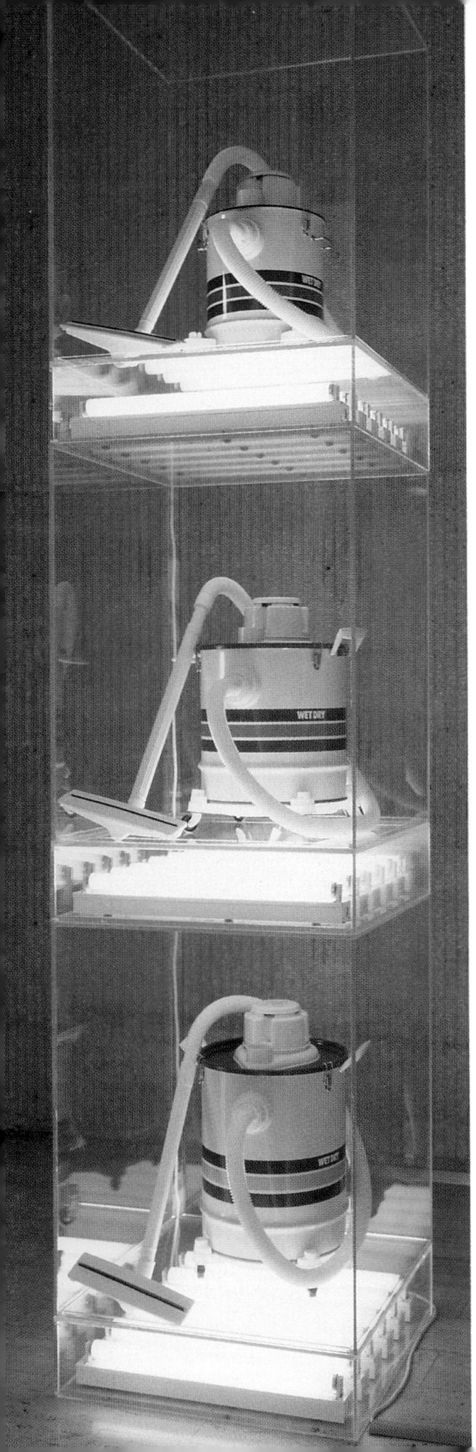

# Beyond Dust

It's hard to imagine life without the vacuum cleaner. Not only has it made keeping up with dust easier, but it has also become a part of our history. Vacuum cleaner maker Black & Decker is so certain of the product's importance that in 1995 the company donated one of the first Dust-busters to the Smithsonian Institution in Washington, D.C.

The Hoover Company has gone a step farther and created its own museum. At the Hoover Historical Center in North Canton, Ohio, visitors can see nearly one hundred different versions of Hoover cleaners through history.

Do you think Black & Decker and Hoover might be exaggerating the importance of the vacuum cleaner just a little bit? Stop and think back to the days when brooms were the only way to clean up dust. If you were growing up during the mid-1800s, sweeping the kitchen *every day* might have been your chore. You might also have had to help with sweeping parlors and other rooms on weekends instead of having a day off to play.

And forget spring vacations! Every year, usually during the last two weeks in April, houses were turned upside down for spring cleaning. Spring cleaning was thorough—and thoroughly disruptive. Women generally did most of the work and dreaded the annual cleaning. But kids probably had fun whacking rugs and carpets with beaters.

Most housekeepers and children probably didn't think much of vacuum cleaners when they saw the first models. Early vacuum cleaners were so heavy they had to be carried on carts. At least two burly men were needed to run them. Eventually, people like Anna Bissell and Murray Spangler helped to make lightweight, affordable carpet sweepers and vacuum cleaners.

*Opposite page: Artist Jeff Koons uses vacuum cleaners in his work. At right: A young girl prepares to help with cleaning chores in the late 1800s, before the invention of the vacuum cleaner.*

*From* Mrs. Doubtfire *to* Hocus Pocus, *the vacuum cleaner has a starring role in our popular culture.*

## Sweeping Changes

Since the days of Booth and Spangler, the vacuum cleaner's role in our society has changed. No longer do vacuum cleaners just help us clean. They're so much a part of our culture that they turn up in books and films as often as they're pulled out of closets.

In David Small's book, *Hoover's Bride,* a homeowner falls in love with a hardworking vacuum cleaner and marries it. Before the invention of the vacuum cleaner, most witches rode brooms. But Kathy Najimy, the third witch in the film *Hocus Pocus,* flies off on a vacuum cleaner.

*Calvin, from the cartoon* Calvin and Hobbes, *takes the war on dust one step farther.*

The vacuum cleaner represents more than an extra job that needs doing. It gives us a way to win the war on dust, and, by cleaning quickly, it gives us time to do other things. Before H. Cecil Booth breathed in dust through his handkerchief, many wives and mothers felt chained to their housework.

Kids benefit from the vacuum cleaner, too. One hundred years ago, you might have spent all weekend cleaning, with no time off to play. So next time you vacuum your room, thank H. Cecil Booth, Murray Spangler, and a long line of inventors. Without their hard work, you'd be stuck beating carpets and curtains. And you'd probably be wheezing yourself to sleep at night.

# Build Your Own Vacuum Cleaner

## You Will Need:

cardboard tube from toilet paper roll

clear, self-adhesive mailing tape, at least 2 inches wide

ruler

sharp pencil

long cardboard tube from wrapping paper, paper towel, or foil roll

sharp knife

scissors

construction paper

thumbtack

wide straw, such as those used at fast-food restaurants

small plastic bag or sandwich bag

1. Cover one end of the toilet paper tube with mailing tape. Firmly press the tape against the walls of the tube to seal. Set tube aside.

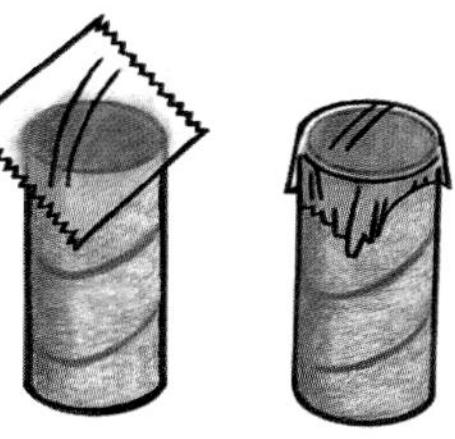

2. Using a ruler and pencil, measure and mark off a 5-inch section of the long cardboard tube. Ask an adult to cut through the wall of the tube with a sharp knife. Discard the rest of the tube or save it to make more vacuum cleaners.

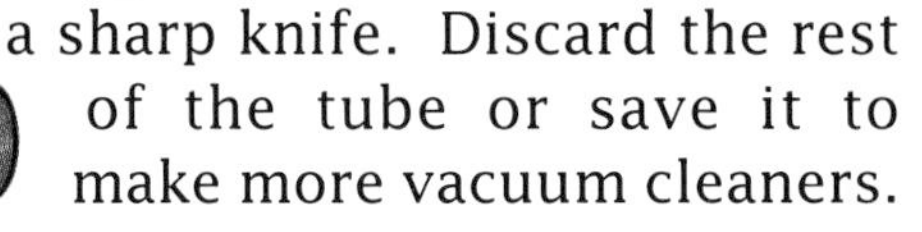


3. Using scissors, cut out a 3-inch square of construction paper and place it on a flat surface. Place the tube section upright on the construction paper. Trace with a pencil around the tube onto the paper. Cut out the circle shape.

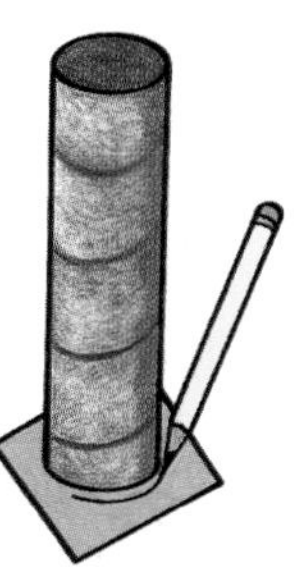

4. Place paper circle over one end of tube section. Cover both the paper and the tube end with mailing tape.

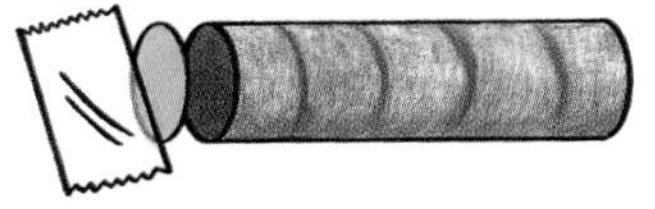

5. Using a thumbtack, poke a hole into the center of the paper and tape covering the tube end. Next push a sharp pencil through the hole, making it big enough to insert a straw. Insert the straw.

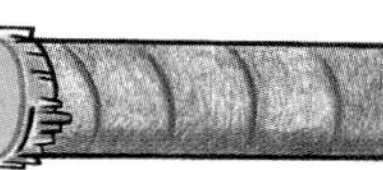

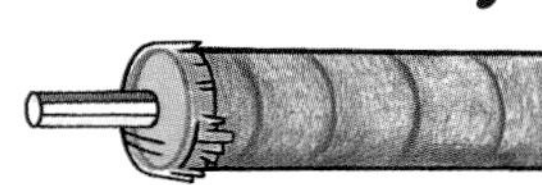

6. Insert the open end of the cardboard tube section into the open end of the toilet paper roll. The tube section should fit snugly just inside the toilet paper roll, with about ½ inch of overlap.

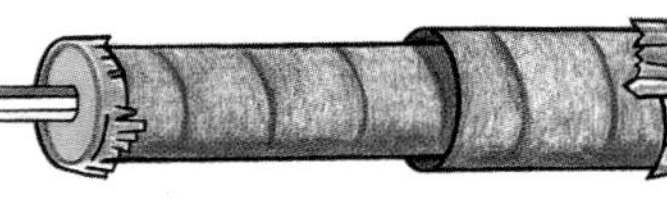

7. Cut along the side and bottom of the plastic bag, opening it up into a rectangle. Place the rectangle of plastic on a flat surface. Place the tubes on top of the plastic bag and roll the bag around them. Tape the bag around the tubes. Then tape the open seam of the bag to seal.

## What Happens:

Push the tubes of your vacuum together so the smaller one fits into the larger one. Then aim the straw at a pile of pepper or salt. With one hand on the larger tube and one on the smaller tube, quickly pull the larger tube back. When you pull back, you create a vacuum. The air pressure inside the tubes is less than the weight of the atmosphere outside the tubes. The difference in air pressure produces suction. Outside air rushes in to fill the vacuum, carrying with it the grains of pepper or salt.

# Glossary

**atmosphere:** while this word has many meanings, in this book it refers to the pressure generated against a surface by air molecules.

**bellows:** a mechanism that can be expanded like a balloon by pulling outward on its handles. Expanding the bellows brings air into a pleated bag. When the handles are pushed together, the bellows forces air out in a great rush.

**"bisselling":** originally, this word meant using a Bissell carpet sweeper to clean rugs and carpets. Because the Bissell sweeper was so popular, people began saying "bisselling" to mean using any brand of carpet sweeper.

**broomcorn:** any one of several types of sorghum grown for the flower clusters which, when dried, are used in making brooms

*Vacuuming with modern cleaners is so easy, in many homes kids vacuum as part of their chores. To prepare for her role as the family vacuumer, this girl in the 1950s uses a toy vacuum to pick up table crumbs.*

**carpet beaters:** a handheld device for whacking rugs and carpets as they hang on a line. Shaped like a large fly-swatter or tennis racket and often made of heavy wire, these beaters knock clouds of dust out of carpets.

**carpet sweeper:** a cleaning machine that uses a revolving brush to push dust and dirt up from floors and carpets and into a dustpan built into the cleaner

**compressed air:** when molecules of air are pumped into a rigid container under pressure, you can squeeze up to 150 times as many molecules into the container as would normally occur. This squeezed-in air is called compressed air. If the container is opened, the air molecules rush out with great force—enough force to drive an engine.

**dust mites:** microscopic creatures that live in mattresses, pillows, and chair or sofa cushions. They look like insects, and they eat the scales of skin that flake off humans every day.

**filter:** a screen or other material that allows one substance (such as air) to pass freely while holding back other particles (such as dust and dirt)

**suction:** the act of pulling air molecules out of one contained space so that the air pressure in that area drops

**vacuum:** the empty space that is left when there are too few air molecules. For example, the space in a straw after you suck out all the liquid and air is a vacuum.

**vacuum cleaner:** a cleaning machine that uses a vacuum created by suction to pull up dust and dirt. Driven by a motor, the hose of a vacuum cleaner, like a straw, sucks up dust-laden air into the cleaner. There, the dirt, dust, and air are pulled into a filter bag. While the air can escape, the dust and dirt are trapped in the bag.

# Index